# LEGENDS OF THE MOUNTAIN MEN

# LEGENDS OF THE MOUNTAIN MEN

## TRISTAN EVERGREEN

# CONTENTS

| | | |
|---|---|---|
| Introduction | | 1 |
| **1** | Chapter 1: The Early Mountain Men | 3 |
| **2** | Chapter 2: Skills and Survival Techniques | 7 |
| **3** | Chapter 3: Encounters with Native American Tribes | 9 |
| **4** | Chapter 4: Expeditions and Discoveries | 13 |
| **5** | Chapter 5: Legends and Folklore | 15 |
| **6** | Chapter 6: Legacy of the Mountain Men | 19 |
| Conclusion | | 21 |

Copyright © 2025 by Tristan Evergreen
All rights reserved. No part of this book may be reproduced in any manner whatsoever without written permission except in the case of brief quotations embodied in critical articles and reviews.
First Printing, 2025

# Introduction

In the annals of North America, few groups are as shrouded in mystery and myth as the mountain men who eked out a romantic, though dangerous, life in the untamed wilderness of the United States and Canada during the 19th century. Epic duels with native trappers, daring sea battles in the arid desert, and relentless thousand-mile horseback chases — these are just a few snippets from the lives of these legendary figures.

These mysteries have spawned countless tall tales and outright fabrications, as numerous as the grains of sand in the deserts where many of these mountain men lived and ultimately perished. In this book, we aim to bring you the real stories, genuine experiences drawn from the writings of men like Joseph Walker, Warren Angus Ferris, Osborne Cross, George Frederick Ruxton, Captain Joseph Pope, John G. McCutchen, and Joseph Meek. These tales — especially those recorded by mountain men like Bezaleel Billingsly, Walter Meachim, and Osborne Cross — have often been locked away in the archives of historical libraries, while others have been published for only a few fortunate readers.

Told in a style and language that many historians find difficult to interpret, these stories gain an air of authenticity through their raw and unembellished recounting. Every man's story is presented here as he told it. As we embark on this journey through the past, there is only one thing missing: the vermin in our coffers and our blackest mood, retelling these tales until the candlelight dims, the shadows lengthen on the wall, and our hearts synchronize in their pulsing with the rhythm of history.

**Purpose and Scope of the Book**

This book contains stories from nearly all the decades of the 19th century west of the Missouri River, serving as an authentic representation of the lives of mountain men like Lewis Wetzel. Covering the very end of the push against the Flathead tribe, this collection offers some of the most compelling and dramatic tales available from that era. The material, though sometimes challenging to work with due to the lack of personal journals, has been pieced together from the few words these men left behind.

While no additional drama has been added by the author, the source material itself is inherently dramatic. Journal keepers of this era did their best to report the essential facts of what they heard and saw, preserving a vivid picture of the past. Over time, spelling and language have naturally evolved, but only minor phonetic corrections have been made to ensure accuracy.

This collection delves deep into the daring and dramatic lives of the mountain men who lived in what are now Wyoming, Idaho, and western Montana. Beyond the legendary stories of Lewis Wetzel, this book also explores the world of Buckskin Joe, the keelboatsman, the wild Indian, the Indian fighter, the hunter, the trapper, the explorer, and the Army scout. These pages bring to life their adventures and the rugged spirit of the American frontier.

**CHAPTER 1**

# Chapter 1: The Early Mountain Men

The early mountain men were a fascinating and diverse group of individuals, each drawn from various stocks of Americans seeking adventure and fortune in the wilderness. Among them was John Colter, who ventured west with the Lewis and Clark expedition in 1804. Colter's story is synonymous with the rugged spirit of exploration, as he later journeyed alone through treacherous territories, laying the groundwork for what would become a legacy of frontiersmen.

Then there was Jedediah (Jed) Smith, who in 1822, along with only eight men, began trapping in the mountainous regions. Smith quickly emerged as a leading figure among the mountain men, famed for his perseverance and adaptability amidst the harshest of challenges. Alongside these American pioneers were Indian trappers, members of various tribes who had invaluable knowledge of the land and survival skills. They were often accompanied by French-Canadian hunters and trappers, known for their deep-rooted traditions in fur trading.

Among these groups were the "free trappers," individuals who roamed the mountains at will, answering to no man. These trappers were often of French-Canadian or American descent, embodying a spirit of independence and resistance to any form of authority. Each group contributed to the rich tapestry of mountain men culture, blending traditions, knowledge, and survival strategies honed over 300 years of frontier expansion across the American East.

Adapting to the way of life in the Rocky Mountains was a seamless transition for many, as their predecessors had already laid the foundation through vigorous frontier expansion. The slow pace of westward expansion meant that it was only recently that Americans came into contact with the Rocky Mountains. The tactics used by early seacoast settlers to gather furs and hides were mirrored by the mountain men, who traded with local tribes in the Missouri and Mississippi River bottoms of present-day Missouri and Arkansas. These interactions allowed them to exchange goods with distant tribes in return for horses and other civilized articles that would be resold later.

**Exploration and Settlement of the American West**

The American West is often associated with exploration, hardship, and the determination of settlers who ventured across vast, uncharted plains seeking new lives and fortunes. The combined forces of European expansion and technological advancement transformed the land into something epic and romantic. Settlers faced numerous natural disasters, including fires, floods, avalanches, and rockslides. This harsh environment meant that any small injury could prove fatal, emphasizing the old adage: "A man's a fool to stay in towns."

The advent of the railroad helped to further transform the nation, causing cities to expand and lands of abundance to shrink. The lure of the "land of the free" drew many to the West. The tales of mountain men exploring the central Rockies, like John Colter, and the Far West, inspired by the Lewis and Clark expedition, painted visions of hope and promise.

Notable among the allure of westward expansion were the gold strikes of north Georgia in 1828, the silver mines of Colorado in 1870, and the Montana gold discoveries of 1863. The most significant period for fur trading spanned from 1810 to around 1840, seeing the United States expand from coast to the Rocky Mountain ranges and eventually the Bering Strait. This era was marked by the pursuit of fur, with the mountain men embodying the adventurous spirit of exploration.

As the eastern lands were divided and claimed, the mountain men rose from obscurity, driven by the relentless pursuit of fortune and survival amidst frost and flame. Their savage pursuits etched tales of daring and resilience into the annals of American history, leaving a lasting legacy of the rugged frontiersmen who shaped the Wild West.

**CHAPTER 2**

# Chapter 2: Skills and Survival Techniques

This chapter examines various encounters with both human adversaries and wild bears, illustrating typical scenarios of mountain life. Through these stories, which have been passed down through generations, we gain a greater understanding of how people survived and thrived in the early West. Dr. Kirk has provided evidence that such tales were often shared around campfires and at gatherings, enriching the oral history of the frontier.

Chapters two through six of this book focus on the attitudes and skills that defined the mountain men. More than just wilderness survival, it was about "thinking like a mountain man" (or a bear). These men were adept at "staying found," always aware of their location and how to utilize the resources at hand. The threats they faced were numerous, ranging from hostile tribes to fearsome wildlife, and they are often depicted as expert trappers, hunters, and animal husbandry practitioners.

Interestingly, many mountain men were skilled gunsmiths, either trained in Europe or the East. Their survival depended heavily on their knowledge of firearms and weaponry, which they honed over years of practical experience. For centuries, in an era of unreliable law enforcement, their skills earned them a reputation as the "troubleshooters" of the frontier.

**Trapping and Hunting**

In their illuminating work, Bob Scofield and Kenneth Redline explore the wild lives of American mountain men, blending archaeology and history. Legends of the Mountain Men sheds light on the lives of 26 real-life trappers and hunters who lived in the rugged wilderness of the Rocky Mountains between 1807 and 1839. Trapping and hunting were vital to these men, sustaining them and providing a unique perspective on their experiences.

As revealed in their journals and written accounts, mountain men were keen observers of geography, geology, flora, fauna, and climatology. They evolved into a unique amalgam of field scientists and naturalists, documenting their findings as they roamed the wilderness.

Their roots were deep in the Appalachian South, and they often arrived on horseback, dressed in "beep-salvation hunter" or "buckskinned woodsman" attire. They used captured Spanish horses and carried with them a mix of regional customs and dialects, though they developed a distinct western colloquialism. For instance, one mountain man in Trinidad described in 1823 how "in the language of the West, nobody shook hands except on the last day of living or leaving," highlighting a soil-rooted tradition and the necessity of freedom.

Beaver trapping and game hunting were more than just industries; they represented a free, untaxed, and unregulated lifestyle that resonated deeply with mountain men. Their untamed pursuits, whether in fur trading or their personal freedoms, created a legacy of independence and resilience.

# CHAPTER 3

# Chapter 3: Encounters with Native American Tribes

We can glean much about the mountain men's interactions with Native American tribes from the very fact that they managed to engage in trade amidst a backdrop of deep-seated hostilities and cultural divides. Trade required a working relationship between vastly different cultures. Among their most formidable enemies were members of the Blackfoot Confederacy in the northern Rockies. The very fact that deadly enemies could come together in trade suggests that these men were capable of putting aside ancient grudges to do business, with each group believing itself superior to the other.

Some historians have doubted the historical accuracy of the mountain man legends that feature violent encounters with savage Indians and powerful Mexican hacendados. Yet the reality was far from the simplistic, friendly exchanges often portrayed. The mountain man-Indian encounter was complex, marked by resistance, accommodation, fear, and mutual dependence. Indian trade could be dangerous, with both parties acutely aware of the ever-present threat of violence.

The Indian trade experience was alienating for the mountain men. Having lost their own culture, they found themselves straddling two worlds—sometimes acting like whites, other times like Indians. Violence was a common language for both mountain men and their Native American counterparts. Vendettas and feuds were part of both societies. In the final analysis, mountain men often found themselves as "lost men," disconnected from their roots and navigating an uncertain existence among the Plains Indians.

**Trade and Conflict**

The interactions between mountain men and Native Americans were a blend of trade and combat. From the traders' perspective, getting Native Americans dependent on their goods was advantageous. While traders sold arms to the Indians, they tried to keep these transactions discreet to prevent intra-tribal warfare. The goal was to gather all the furs that different tribes wouldn't exchange amongst themselves.

Notable traders like Ashley and Smith played crucial roles in introducing mountain men to various Native American tribes. For example, A.D. Ferris views Ashley as not unkind to the Crow, who were quite self-sufficient. Ashley once used Charbonneau as a translator to facilitate communication. This interpersonal dynamic speaks volumes about the delicate balance between trade and conflict.

The Hudson's Bay Company (HBC) expressed their disdain for mountain men like Jedediah and William, yet their lucrative dealings often forced them to compromise, even when Ashley auctioned his pelts for better prices than the Arikara tribes.

Mountain men highlighted their resilience and resourcefulness by loading pack saddles with ashes and dumping lemons off mules. An HBC clerk lamented that his people were "the worst selection from the orphans of London." Explorers like Ferris and Warren Ferris introduced mountain men to trade partners, where they bartered beaver pelts in exchange for valuable goods, often destroying surplus resources to maintain market stability.

The Crow had a mixed relationship of war and peace with neighboring tribes. When they sold game to a tribe, they respected the arrangement and refrained from hunting that game for someone else. Even the Crows and Snakes maintained a peace footing while hunting in shared territories. However, following a war, hostile encounters were inevitable, where an unsuspecting traveler could be met with a "friendly arrow" from a previously friendly face.

Accounts from the Hidatsa highlight the care and craftsmanship that went into making bows and arrows, ensuring that they were both effective and stealthy. Arrows from ancient times were shorter than those used in later periods. Discoveries of four such ancient arrows in willow brush demonstrated the skill and tradition passed down through generations.

# CHAPTER 4

# Chapter 4: Expeditions and Discoveries

The mountain men played a significant role in pushing the western border of the United States to the Continental Divide and beyond. In the summer of 1824, Jedediah Smith made a groundbreaking discovery when he explored South Pass—a critical, easy passage to the Pacific waters. The existence of this pass not only paved the way for a continental railroad but also accelerated the opening of the entire West to settlers and explorers.

Eight years later, Smith and Thomas Fitzpatrick guided a Santa Fe trade caravan westward and over the Divide. Their assertion that wagons could traverse this route was instrumental in initiating the great western migration, which eventually led to the acquisition of California. Although hunting was important to the mountain men, they were neither solely fur trappers nor big game hunters. Unlike fur companies, these men did not deplete an area of its resources before moving on. Instead, they hunted across dozens of valleys and explored countless mountain ranges, frequently discovering furs by circumstance.

Countless trappers joined small hunting parties, discovering rivers and mountains previously traversed only by native tribes and an occasional fur brigade. Before the fur trappers, the Northwest had seen the establishment of Astor's fur trading posts along the West Coast, and explorers like David Thompson had ventured into the interior valleys. However, vast tracts of North America north of Mexico remained an enigma to both the U.S.A and the wider world. These expeditions were critical in charting the geography of the unexplored Rocky Mountain region, significantly contributing to our understanding of this vast territory.

**Mapping the Uncharted Territories**

The mountain men who undertook the task of mapping the uncharted territories of the western United States performed an invaluable service by bringing unknown lands, creatures, and peoples into the geographical consciousness of humanity. Their recorded travels and observations documented places previously identified only by Native American names, transforming them into well-known geographic locations.

The Rocky Mountains represented the first barrier to the westward expansion of America. Mountain men, including "Ashley's Hundred," were instrumental in discovering and recognizing suitable routes through the Rockies, such as the one located by Lewis and Clark and later Jedediah Smith. Unlike the more ordered exploration missions of the U.S. government, fur traders and trappers often followed ancient Indian routes delineated by the movements of fur-bearing animals. Their natural curiosity frequently led them to cross headwaters ridges to discover new streams and landscapes beyond.

This Alpine wall, referred to as the "great backbone," stretched 3,000 miles and presented a series of challenges for these untutored explorers to conquer. By mapping these uncharted territories, they provided invaluable knowledge that helped shape the United States' expansion westward.

**CHAPTER 5**

# Chapter 5: Legends and Folklore

As the mountain men passed from history into memory, their legends and folklore began to permeate the mountains where they lived and roamed. Their heritage unfolded in the eyes and outlook of the West, with tales often spun by old mountaineers recounting their adventures around campfires. These stories, passed down through generations, often found themselves woven into the fabric of Western lore.

Among these tales is the St. Vrain legend, a story that has been shared since at least 1957. It may have originated from some old mountaineer sitting on the Sunny Slope Ranch north of what is now Durango, Colorado. These campfire yarns were in the tradition of the old Dutchman found among the Indian tribes, interpreting for the Spaniards in New Mexico, and later serving as scouts after the Louisiana Purchase. The descendants of the Indians likely intermarried with the descendants of the old Dutchman, stretching the legend to fit the mountain men's history as told by other white men.

These legends and beliefs, even in their fanciful forms, reveal the attitudes and resilience of the mountain men. They highlight our basic humanity, the struggle against difficulties, and the occasional triumphs despite the obstacles and dangers that often elude historians, anthropologists, and folklorists. Perhaps one day, tangible facts may surface to authenticate the mountain men as cultural heroes embedded in our modern folklore.

### Tales of Bravery and Resilience

One such legend is that of "Black" Harris, a story many children in Colorado grew up hearing. Harris, a mountain man who guided exploring scientists through remote sections of the high country, single-handedly saved them when a surprise snowstorm trapped them beneath heavy drifts. Trekking over a hundred miles across the winter wonderland, the daring animal tracker managed to guide help to the site—two weeks after the calamitous event.

The legend has since become somewhat muddied with the historical narrative. Hastings White, assistant director of the Denver Museum of Nature and Science, along with fellow scientists, were snowbound in North Park during the winter of 1913–14. Harris returned from a jaunt with sixty miles worth of news to Waller in four days, bearing weighty importance about his companions and their prospect of death. Dan Waller, a seasoned mountain guide who earned fame similar to Harris in the following years of his career, subsequently set out to the scene and salvaged the entomologists, arriving at the site after an arduous mountain pass march, just under a week after leaving the trailhead at Rawah.

The folklore of the Rocky Mountains is filled with tales of mountain men forged from a unique alloy of bravery and resilience. These stories highlight the tenacity with which they calmly confronted the wild, allowing the best of pulp traditions to come to the fore. A rich tapestry of prose about the incredible circumstances real rural folk, trappers, prospectors, and travelers often experienced as they set out across hostile foothills and deserts, intent on making rugged lives for themselves.

Whether these accounts come directly from travelers or circulate as varied and circuitous anecdotes, they offer a true sense of classic storytelling. These tales have stood the test of time, providing insight into the indomitable spirit of the mountain men and the enduring fascination they hold in our collective imagination.

**CHAPTER 6**

# Chapter 6: Legacy of the Mountain Men

Understanding the sources behind this exploration is crucial. We draw on Shea's work, Richard Mabey's Beechcombings, Bernd Heinrich's Winter World, David Quammen's The Song of the Dodo, Ralph Acampora's Corporal Compassion, and Holling's various papers. Shea also has a conference paper from 2001 on this topic, which is available on his website and might provide further insights.

**The Ennobling Wilderness** details how the experiences of the mountain men heavily influenced their lives and character. Most strikingly, despite their varied outcomes as respectable citizens, recluses, outcasts, or persistent mountain men, they shared a profound respect for nature and wild places that set them apart. Their time among the untamed seemed to enlighten and ennoble them in a rough, colloquial manner. They returned to society with a sense of belonging to the world, which others found wondrous and inspiring. Their excursions into the wilderness opened doors and warmed hearts.

It's important to reflect on the power of nature in shaping character. The impact of the mountain wilderness on these men was profound. Their rough and often wretched experiences in the wild played a significant role in their development, making them more open and outwardly focused. This understanding of the environment's role in personal growth is fundamental when adapting practices or philosophies to new places.

**Influence on American Culture**

The mountain men have been immortalized in countless ways throughout American culture, including in artwork, souvenirs, careers, campgrounds, trading posts, historical monuments, and more. Their exploits were popularized in the "dime novels" of the 1800s, and Hollywood brought the mountain man to life in films such as The Big Sky. Many museums scattered across the western U.S. feature artifacts, documents, and artwork from that era, preserving the legacy of these rugged individuals.

Names like Paul Bunyan, Hugh Glass, Jedediah Smith, Kit Carson, Jim Bridger, and John Colter have left a lasting imprint on American culture. These figures have been the subjects of numerous books and scholarly works, highlighting their significance in history. Today, thousands of reenactors annually recreate the life and times of the mountain men in the American West during events and gatherings.

In many national parks, one can visit sites where mountain men trapped, traded, or hunted. The Santa Fe Trail in Missouri follows the path of these pioneers, and the rendezvous site in Wyoming remains a popular tourist destination. The lifestyle of the real mountain men continues to be a rich subject for historical study and public fascination.

**CONCLUSION**

# Conclusion

The stories of the mountain men still capture our attention and linger in our souls, forming an essential part of American heritage. Their hardships and adventures inspire us during tough times, offering warnings, insights, and a unique perspective on the civilizations they helped to create. Reflecting on these men brings thoughts of courage, risk, thrills, and compensation—a grand saga of wilderness adventure, societal development, and life's unparalleled education.

These tales speak of men who navigated their way through the wilderness, facing relentless struggles at every twist and turn of the sinewy trails. The hardships were unending for the trappers. Yet, the quiet compensation was found in the grand solitude that mirrored the wilderness of their souls. Common men like Chief Joseph lived at peace with themselves, facing profound dangers in places like the Green Hell of the Blackfeet Indian Empire, Yellowstone, and the rich buffalo country of Wyoming and Montana.

**Reflections on the Mountain Men's Impact**

Mountain men did exist, and their lives were as heroic, brutal, and fascinating as the characters portrayed in movies—perhaps even more so. At Yellowstone Press, we hope to rekindle some of the qualities and values of these men in their direct descendants—us, we, and you—who still have much to learn from their lives, choices, and experiences.

For a brief generation or two, maybe even four, mountain men roamed the mostly untouched and unspoiled West. Up through the 1930s, the mountain men were more than just memories; their existence was recorded in documents, oral histories of Indian tribes, cache sites of their belongings, and the few places they visited. The period of the mountain men defines a significant part of our history: the permanent occupation of the far West, the increase of overland travel, and the expansion of wilderness trails that allowed people to move through that God-given preserve and pastureland. They explored and trapped in remote, untouched wilderness areas.

We hope that their legacy and spirit will subtly and indelibly influence you. Our further hope is that you will sell many books, allowing us to write more about these incredible adventurers. Together, the mountain men—"the original extreme outdoor adventure athletes"—will continue to capture our hearts. That's how we got here, and that's why Mountain Men—a book with a long history in production and a short history in actuality—will enter the market with confidence, forever fascinating those who admire these bravest of the brave and most reckless of the reckless, as Jim Bridger declared of his breed in 1870.

www.ingramcontent.com/pod-product-compliance
Lightning Source LLC
LaVergne TN
LVHW042156070526
838201LV00047BA/1542